SEO
Marketing

*How To Rank #1 When You
Are Just An Average Joe*

By

Alain Magnuson

Table of Contents

Introduction...*1*

Chapter 1 ....*3*

   Importance Of Seo For Your Website................................*3*

Chapter 2 ....*6*

   Why Can't Search Engines Work Without Seo?................*6*

Chapter 3 ....*9*

   Importance Of Traffic Trap *9*

Chapter 4 ....*12*

   Finding The Right Keywords *12*

Chapter 5 ....*15*

   Crafting Your Content...*15*

Chapter 6 ....*33*

   The Difference Between On-Page Seo Vs. Off-Page Seo .*33*

Chapter 7 ....*61*

   Perks Of Off-Page Seo...*61*

Chapter 8 ....*72*

   Earning Through Blogging *72*

Chapter 9 ....*76*

   Amazon Affiliate Marketing And Seo...........................*76*

Chapter 10 ....*86*

   Writing Search-Optimized Review Articles...................*86*

INTRODUCTION

❧

SEO – Love it or hate it, but at the end of the day, you're still going to need it.

The term 'SEO' is used widely within the online marketing industry, and there is a good reason why: Put quite simply, in the world of online marketing, you need SEO to survive.

Let's face it, we see and hear people say 'SEO' all the time, especially online entrepreneurs, however, there are not a lot of people who actually know how to gain good rankings on Google.

Don't worry, it doesn't mean that to get your site listed on the top page of search engines you're going to need take a four-year degree course.

While it's true that there are some 'online gurus' who claim to have studied SEO for a decade, and call themselves 'pro's' in the industry, most of those 'experts' are not exactly what you think they are.

We can't deny the fact that mastering all the aspects of SEO, and putting them into context, might take some time, however, the good news is that when it comes to learning about the fundamentals, you can actually get them down in a single day.

CHAPTER 1

～

Importance of SEO for Your Website

Even if you're new to this whole SEO charade, I'd bet you already know that most web traffic is commonly driven by the big three search engines - Google, Bing, and, of course, Yahoo!

Sure, social media, and the like, are able to drive traffic to your website – and they are an important factor – but focusing on search engines is your primary goal as they are the means of navigation for most people.

This is true for every business out there, regardless of whether your website delivers content, services, information, or something else. The fact is, you need SEO.

Search engines are quite unique. They lead the right people to your website; what you might call 'targeted traffic'. These are the people who are ready to purchase, or who are at least interested in buying in what you are offering.

You could say that search engines are considered the roadways that make the internet come to life. So, if your site isn't SEO-friendly, the search engines won't easily find and highly rank your content, which means you won't be getting traffic – well, you might, but you will be missing out on substantial visitor traffic and the incredible opportunities such traffic offers.

Now, talk about search queries – these are the words, or 'keywords' people type into the search engine when they're trying to find something.

As an online marketer, you need to know that keywords have extraordinary value. Experience and other data have clearly shown that search engine traffic, gained by using the right keywords, can do one of two things: It can make OR break a company's financial success.

The importance of targeted traffic involves three things: The delivery of publicity, of revenue, and finally, of exposure. These three things are likely to give carry weight when they are generated by your targeted traffic. No other type of marketing can outdo this.

Investing time, money, and effort on learning about the ins and outs of SEO will provide a lot of advantages for your company when compared to other types of marketing, specifically as they apply to online (or offline) promotion.

CHAPTER 2

~

Why Can't Search Engines Work Without SEO?

We can all agree that search engines are smart, but that doesn't mean they can do everything. While it's true that search engines are evolving at an incredible pace, and that their algorithms change quite often, we're still at the point where they need a bit more 'push' to help them find what you have to offer.

Current technology allows us to probe deeply into the World Wide Web, with Google, so far, taking the lead in providing better results for users.

However, this doesn't change the fact that current technology is still limited. Using the right ways to manipulate SEO can give you a lot of benefits, such as an increased drive in traffic, but if you don't do it correctly, then you might easily achieve the opposite reaction to what you want.

Get it wrong and your site will be buried deep down in the far reaches of the search engines, along with billions of others. So, you can effectively say goodbye to your traffic because no one is going to find your content, regardless of how informative it is.

Doing SEO Alone – Is It Possible?

Although I have mentioned that the fundamentals of SEO are quite simple to understand, the world of SEO is quite complex. Focusing on the basics will be an easy ride for you though.

The thing with SEO is that even if you only have a small amount of knowledge, but you use it the right way, it can actually make a big difference to your traffic.

As a matter of fact, SEO education is readily available on the internet, for example, this e-Book you're reading right now.

If you're going to take this seriously and truly understand what I have to say, and ally that with constant practice, you will have nothing to worry about.

It really depends on the time you have to give, your commitment, and your willingness to learn. Of course, the complexity of your website can also contribute to how fast or how slow you can go to the top of the search engines.

If you don't have enough time to work on SEO, or you're only in it for the big picture, then you would be better advised to hire someone to do it for you.

In any case, reading this guide will give you an informed insight into what you're faced with.

CHAPTER 3

❧

Importance of Traffic Trap

I can't stress enough how big a mistake marketers' make when they only look at SEO as a means of getting free traffic – sure, we're after the free traffic but that's not how SEO operates.

Here's what I want you to think: **SEO is all about helping prospective clients, who are searching for you, to find you.** To achieve the desired goal, your website, and all the contents in it, must match what people are searching for.

Example:

Elena owns a site that sells knitted sweaters. On the website, Elena creates posts about how she makes her knitted sweaters by hand. Usually, she writes about the variety of yarns she uses.

The keyword 'yarn' doesn't have a lot of competition within search engines. Because of this, and Elena's consistency in posting high-quality content on the subject, several of her pages are ranked high on the first page of Google for different types of yarn.

So, what's the potential problem?

While it's a good thing that Elena's content has generated traffic through her posts, it's going to be a problem in the long-run as her primary goal is to market her custom-made knitted sweaters.

People who are typing away on search engines, looking for different types of yarn, are most likely knitting for themselves. In other words, they won't be very interested in purchasing Elena's sweaters.

Elena will surely receive a lot of traffic, but it's completely useless to have traffic that doesn't convert. Basically, visitors to Elena's site are searching for a completely different purpose.

Take Note:

To make SEO work for you, you have to ensure your goals, as an entrepreneur, are in sync with the objectives of your visitors. It's never about the traffic alone; it's about trying to figure out what you want to achieve and making it easy to meet with the people who are looking for the same thing.

How do you make sure you're using the right keywords?

The answer is easy: Research.

…. which leads me to the next topic.

CHAPTER 4

Finding the Right Keywords

Researching keywords can be quite tiring. It's a long, unavoidable process that you have to go through to find the right keywords for your niche. Basically, the ideal keywords that you're looking for conform to the following:

- They must have a high search volume – there should be people searching for the indicated keywords
- They must have low competition – having a small competition quotient increases your chances of ranking higher
- They must be supported by the content you post – keywords should be relevant to your website

Looking for the right keywords may not be as random as you think as there are a lot of tools already on the market you can use. Currently, Google's Search-Based Keyword tool is at the top of its game. It's heavily used by online marketers because of its accuracy.

This tool delivers results that are based on real-time Google searches, and if you log in into your AdWords account, the tool will automatically give you a list of a keyword of ideas you can incorporate in your content for customization.

Let's stop there for a moment and talk about the decision you have to make on how broad, or narrow, you plan to make your keywords. This is what is referred to as, 'Long Tail'.

The Long Tail

The popularity of long tail rose when Chris Anderson decided to take action. Long tail happens when a lot of low traffic keywords are able to, collectively, provide you with more traffic than a couple of high-traffic keywords on their own can.

Example:

Amazon usually receives thousands of visits from clients with the keyword, 'DVD', however, Amazon receives millions of visits coming searchers looking for the individual titles of DVD's (i.e., Spiderman, Kung Fu Panda, etc.)

Naturally, the number of visit per title searched does not come close to the keyword 'DVD', but the tables are turned when we use long tail keywords – the volume is way higher than only one keyword.

What's in it for you?

The moment you combine all your long tail – in other words unpopular – keywords, it should dominate your page visits, attracting approximately 80% of your traffic.

I'm mentioning this because new marketers often make the grave mistake of focusing on one keyword that carries crazy amounts of traffic. There are times when you have to focus on the long tail keywords that aren't popular and use them in your content to create your strategy.

CHAPTER 5

⌒

Crafting Your Content

Keywords always come first as they'll form the basis of your content, and you must know them before you can start writing. Once they've been established, it's time to make some content magic.

Every search engine has 'bots' (short for robots) that have been programmed to crawl all over your website. They do this to find out what your content is all about. After they've examined your site and content, these bots decide what the keywords for your page are and where it should rank.

In your own way, you can manipulate the bots' decision by thoroughly optimizing your content for specific keywords that you want to be known for.

This is even more true if you fancy publishing content bots aren't able to decipher. Sure, interpreting text is child's play for bots, but we just aren't there yet in terms of technology to decipher your content through videos, pictures, and audio.

This means you have to describe everything in a way that bots are able to understand so they can rank your page with the use of the correct keywords.

Warning

Focusing all your content for search engines on keywords will make your content boring and, although you may get a lot of traffic from your searches, your conversions will remain low. Make people the priority rather than search engines. Write the way you speak, and optimize your content here, there and everywhere.

Please note; right now I'm only going to briefly explain the fundamentals. We'll dig deeper into the subject later.

Titles

The titles in your content should be eye-catching enough to pique the interest of your readers.

Remember: **You only have one chance to make a first impression.**

In creating the titles of your content, there's no such thing as a one-size-fits-all kind of answer on the length they should be. It greatly depends on what the goals are you're trying to achieve, and where will your headline show up.

If you're focusing on making sure your post is ranking and banking in the search engines, then you would have to make your title at least fewer than 70 characters to prevent cut off in the results pages.

However, it's a different story if your goal is to gain popularity on social media. According to a HubSpot analysis, headlines between eight to twelve words in length are shared more often on Twitter than other headlines.

On Facebook, headlines need to be around twelve to fourteen words to receive 'likes'.

Keywords

Choose keywords that are relevant and that are going bring people to your page.

Links

Do you obtain information for your content from any other site? If you have, you must not forget to link them to your content from time to time (these 'information' sites should be grade A informants).

This will encourage websites within your niche to reach out to you in return.

Quality

Focus on publishing contents that are unique and high in quality. Spending more time than usual crafting your content will encourage readers of your site to stick around as high-quality content is hard to come by.

Freshness

There are times when we create content that doesn't age, but that only rarely happens. Most of the time, the contents we create requires you to constantly add new information or keep updated on a monthly basis.

If you're one of those people who is working to a busy schedule, and your website isn't earning enough to hire someone to update content for you, then you can always update your blog by putting a question on your site and including a section for answers.

Even though updating your website is important, you must NEVER steal content from other peoples' sites. Search engines will find the duplicate content and you can be penalized for plagiarism.

Headings

Headings on a website are quite similar to book headings with one slight difference – they come in a specific order. They follow the sequence that runs H1, H2, H3, and so on.

Naturally, H1 is the headline that begins the page as the blog heading. As for the rest, they descend down to the lower headings of your page.

Here's an example:

<h1>SEO Marketing for Beginners</h1>
<h2>The 123 of Learning SEO</h2>
<h3>Research</h3>

Notice the pattern of the headings. If you're going to write content that's more specific and in-depth, then the number of your headings will be higher.

In a nutshell, you're only going to need one H1 tag per page. However, you can have as many more headings as you want.

Note: For better search engine results, the headings should contain keywords that are relevant to the content of your site.

Sitemaps

Sitemaps are like roadmaps made for search engines. Basically, they deliver bots directions to the many different pages found on your website, ensuring that searchers will be able to find everything they need.

There are two types of sitemaps that you will need to create:

- HTML sitemaps
- XML sitemaps

Let's look at the main difference between the two sitemaps. The thing is, XML sitemaps are coded specially for the search engines to understand or read.

On the other hand, HTML sitemaps are both easy for the search engines and people to read. You'll be able to link out to them, which means the visitor will have a clear overview of the pages they visit.

If your site is fairly new, and contains a couple of hundred pages, then you would need to put a link for each page in the HTML sitemap.

On the other hand, if your website has a couple of thousand pages, or more, just determine the most important pages and link out to them.

XML sitemaps will show every single page of your website – yup, even if you have MILLIONS of pages on your website. There are convenient tools to help you out, for example, XML Sitemap Creator, to instantly make a sitemap for your site.

As soon as your XML sitemap is available, you need to pass it to Google Webmaster Central and Bing. This will give you an advantage as the major search engines are able to crawl and index the website.

Domain Name

It turns out that domain names containing keywords are doing better in the rankings than those without any keywords. In fact, domain names that are similar have the tendency to rank higher.

But this comes with a catch: Similar domain names aren't the most unique of their kind. You may have noticed, there are a lot of existing companies using 'made-up' words for their domain names. Doing this gives them the chance to create a brand around the name, instead of having to deduce what the meaning is.

Question: Which is better?
Answer: It varies.

It usually depends on where your traffic comes from. Let's say the traffic you generate comes from search engines. If that's the case, then it would be better for you to use an exact match domain name as it would be more beneficial for you.

Here's an example:

Food.com and computer.com will always have an advantage for the keywords 'Food' and 'Computer'. In this situation, having a keyword rich domain will work better for you.

On the other hand, if you're not really focusing on SEO, or it's only a small part of your strategy, then it would be wiser to go for something unique.

Going back to more than a decade ago, no one was really looking for 'Google', but after they carefully built the brand, it has become the go-to site for everyone – well, almost everyone. It's the same for Zappos and Zillow.

URL Structure

Another factor that is commonly overlooked by online marketers concerns the URL structure as part of SEO. You need to keep your URL's neatly organized and structured or the search engines are going to have a difficult time finding and crawling them.

If search engines have a hard time crawling your pages, they won't be able to successfully index your website. So regardless of how awesome your content is, your page will likely rank lower in the search engines.

Here is a list of factors to remember to ensure that your URL structure is pro search engine.

- URL's should ideally exclude any extraneous characters, such as $, @, !*, %, =, and ?.
- Shorter URL's usually have a better chance of ranking than longer URL's.
- Only numbers and letters should be applied in URL's

- Underscores are big red flags. Search engines rank you higher when you use dashes.
- Sub-domains may rank higher than the sub-directories

Site Structure

Your site structure also dictates how well your page will rank. In other words, how you link your web pages creates a big impact on your search engine rankings.

I've listed a couple of tips for when you cross-link your website:

- Links found within the content are more important than links that are placed on a sidebar or footer as content carries more weight
- If possible, you should ensure the number of links per page is under a hundred
- You should go for no-follow links that aren't relevant to your content (links that do not have high-quality work). For instance, links that go to a Feedburner page.

Some SEO practitioners advocate no-following internal links. An example would be their terms of service. However, the problem with this is that page rank sculpting no longer works.

If you do want to block out pages, like the terms of service, then it would be best for you to do this, so that you could exclude it in the robots.txt file.

Alt Tags

Alt tags are another important factor if you want bots to properly index your images. For this to work in your favor, you need to include alt tags, for each image, together with a brief description of what the picture entails.

For instance, if it is a picture of a computer, I would convey to the search engine that the image is actually a computer through the use of an alt tag. Now, when I do this, it would turn out something like so:

<img src="http://quicksprout.com/images/computer.jpg" alt="computer" />

Naturally, you have to make sure that an image is relevant to its name. If you were uploading an image of a computer to add to your content, you should call it 'computer.jpg' rather than 'image4.jpg'.

Links

Among the things that I've listed in this section, links are probably the most important when it comes to SEO. Imagine this: If there are a lot of websites linking to your site, then it will mean your page will rank higher.

The reason links tend to have a high value in the SEO game is that it would be easy for anyone to research, change their content, or make one in general, BUT, it's a different story when it comes to persuading other websites to link out to you.

Search engines tend to trust websites when there are a lot of other sites that are linking out to them. The sites must be non-spammy for search engines to acknowledge them. The more 'quality' sites that are linking to your page, the higher you would rank in the search engine.

- It would be impossible, in this book, to share everything about building links, however, there are some things you have to know.
- Links should be within the content. This is more effective than when you place them in a sidebar or footer

- Linking sites that are relevant to your content is more effective than links coming from non-related sites
- Anchor text has an important role when it comes to link building. If you want your page to rank for the keyword 'computer', for example, you would need the anchor text of the link to be 'computer' and nothing else.

There are a number of things that you have to avoid:

- Links that are coming from spammy and irrelevant sites will do more harm than good to your rankings
- Site-wide links aren't effective and can hurt your SEO
- Making all of your links rich in anchor text does not give you a head's up in the SEO game
- Reciprocal links aren't effective (This is when you link to a certain site and it links back to you).
- Purchasing text links will get you banned from search engines if you get caught

Here are a number of ways you can increase the count of your link:

Social Media – works in many ways, and if you go on sites like Digg or StumbleUpon, it will give you a lot of traffic, AND it will also help increase your visibility. This means the chances of your site getting linked to becomes higher.

Directories – There are a ton of directories you can find on the internet. You need to take time to submit your site to the relevant ones; the ones that actually compliment, or relates to, your content.

The Top 100 – Let's say your goal is to rank for a specific keyword. The the best links you can find will come from sites that are already part of the big 100 search results for that particular keyword.

Of course, there are some sites that may rank for the keyword that are actually your competitors within your niche. Don't expect them to link to you as it would be a negative thing for them to do.

However, you're going to be surprised how some competitors will link out to your site if you ask them nicely. It doesn't hurt to shoot them a nice e-mail asking for a link out.

Forums – There are a lot of forums on the web that enable you add a signature which you'll be able to link back to your site. It will only work if the links aren't 'no-followed', and it will boost your rankings.

Competition – Probably the easiest way you can get links is to look at the sites that are linking to your competition and contact them via e-mail. Your message should list the benefits of what your website has in comparison to the competition.

Although it's a small number, 5% of the sites you contact will link to your website. So the more people you message, the higher the number of the sites that'll link out to you.

Dead links – If there are millions of active links on the web, then also there are BILLIONS of dead links on the web. You need to realize that a good number of links will die over time.

Websites may go down, while a lot of the links that are directing to them are still alive and kicking. Be smart and e-mail those websites. Tell them about the dead links, and that you have the same content, or operate in the same niche, as the dead site. By doing so, there's a high probability they'll replace the previous link to one that goes to your website.

Implementing everything I have said above will increase traffic. However, you need to be patient. Search engines need time to update their records (since they have to crawl BILLIONS of other sites before they reach yours).

It's also important to keep in mind that figuring out what works for your site may be different from what works for other sites. There's no secret way to get ahead of your competitors other than by doing things right.

Don't attempt to use shady methods to beat your competitors. The algorithms of search engines have undergone great changes in recent years. You will be caught, and your site will be penalized.

White Hat vs. Black Hat

In the field of SEO, you have two choices, do you want to do it for long term or short term? Do you just want some additional pocket money, or do you want to turn it into a stable source of income?

If you want to earn money as soon as possible, or operate some get-rich-quick scheme using SEO, then what you want to know more about is named 'Black Hat SEO'.

SEO black hat basically means that every post you put out is designed to attract search engines but without any special attention for human readers.

You should understand that Black Hat offers several effective ways of making sure your sites are on the top page of google, thus earning somewhat faster. However, when you use any of those ways, you are basically walking a thin line between the right and wrong creation of SEO.

Although this may sound pleasing for beginners, after all, everyone wants to generate money in the fastest way; be warned that taking shortcuts can lead to consequences. To give you an idea of what these consequences might be, then you must understand that by cheating to get your site ranked on the first page, you would be creating 'spam' pages which do not last long.

SEO has now become more prominent since Google heightened their security. Getting caught using black hat methods means grave punishment. Sometimes Google can mete out punishment that would lead you to say goodbye to your plans of making long-term sites.

However, no matter how tight a security system is, there will always be loopholes. You just need to be careful and clever, and you can earn a couple of thousand dollars!

On the other hand, White Hat SEO is the building of supremacy in your online business. A business you plan to nurture for a long period of time. This means the content you create is high-quality text targeting human readers.

The content should always be accessible to everyone and should be in accordance with the rules for ranking.

I would focus on White Hat SEO more. After all, if you really want success in the SEO world, White Hat is the way to go.

CHAPTER 6

∽

The Difference Between On-Page SEO vs. Off-Page SEO

On-Page SEO and Off-Page SEO are the two categories that you must be proficient with.

So, let me give you the basics, when you are dealing with On-Page SEO, the focal point is to develop a page that favors Google's ranking requirements; like headlines, your content, and of course, your page structure.

Alternatively, Off-page SEO basically focuses on every area a search engine looks at. You don't handle this step by step, it is very much dependent on other things like social networkers, other well-ranking blogs in a similar industry, and other personal factors.

If you want to know which of the two is more important, well, let me tell you, it is impossible to make that determination since On-Page SEO and Off-Page SEO are two very different things. Both are extremely important and have a significant impact. So, if you want to succeed, you need to master both categories.

Of course, I want to make things easier for you, so let me give you an idea using a scenario:

Imagine you own a snappy looking boutique selling all the latest fashion trends – from parka jackets, used in the New York Fashion week, to the sheer gowns used by the top models in Milan. Basically, you have the products to offer, and you have done everything to radiate good vibes on your store site.

Scenario No. 1: Your boutique carries all the original, high-quality fashion products, but it looks like a den of illegal smugglers from the outside.

So in this picture, you have the best products on the market, but still offer them at cheaper prices compared to other stores.

The only problem is that the boutique structure looks as if it was built hastily. It appears shady, and, instead of selling high fashion items, it looks like a place of monkey business.

No matter how great the products are, nobody would think a place is credible if it has a shaggy outside appearance.

The same applies if you've created a well-written page that comes with an amazing impact and high-quality content, but nobody is attracted to visit the page. Basically, you got the best page out there, but nobody gives a damn. No traffic means no incoming money.

Scenario No. 2: Your store's breathtaking design and structure can be featured in a magazine. However, you're selling low-quality items at a sky-high price.

Even though this scenario is different to the first, the result is still the same. Sure, the structure might attract a lot of people into visiting your store, however, when they check the items being sold, and the price tags that come with them, they would be out of the store faster than you can say hello.

Again, this would also apply to your online page. When someone checks your website, and only takes a quick glance at one of your pages and exit the window in less than a few minutes, then Google automatically counts that as a bounce.

This is something you would want to steer clear of. If you have a high bounce rate, Google will lower your ranking.

And trust me, that's a sure way to fail.

Do you understand now how essential it is to be proficient with both on-page and off-page SEO?

You can start by focusing right on your page before you start tackling the outside variables. There are still so many things to cover, but let's look at mastering On-Page SEO first.

Going Big on On-Page SEO

For easy comprehension, I've emphasized the three biggest categories when it comes to On-Page.

Content

As someone who has been around in the SEO field for quite a long time, I have learned it is absolutely vital to focus on the content.

Have you heard the phrase 'Content is King'? If you have worked in the SEO field you would have, sooner or later, encountered this phrase. Bill Gates made this statement back in 1996, and many years later, it has become a phrase that speaks the truth in so many avenues in life and business.

But why is content really valued? Simple. Google has designed its search engine to filter and provide high-quality results as much as possible so that their users are happy with what they find on the top page.

Let's say you're looking for 'how to fix a leaking faucet'. Google would perform the magic and make sure the results on the first page are filled with articles that are backed up by reliable sources.

That's generally how Google's algorithm works, in this case, as you soon as enter the keywords, it gives you a list of sites where you can learn how to fix that leaking faucet.

Google is the researcher's friend. It tries its best to make fact-finding easier for anyone who's looking for quality content among the thousands, or millions, of sites that contain the same keyword.

To make it simple, if you want to increase your prospect of ranking high on Google, then you should keep working on including content that is worth reading so your page will be recognized by Google's algorithm.

This means, of course, you must give it your best shot every time. It will take a lot of effort to make it work.

You see, SEO is pretty much the same as mastering other skills in life. As Dwayne Johnson once said, "Success isn't always about greatness. It's about consistency. Consistent hard work leads to success".

Remember though, even if you have the best marketing strategy in the world, it won't help you if you're selling a low-quality product.

Even if you use an advanced SEO skill set, but your content isn't high-quality, then you're nowhere near success.

A successful page would have content that is basically useful and well researched.

Let us tackle the factors that would create awesome content that would elevate you to the top ranks on the search pages of Google.

Quality

Quality products and service are always a game changer in any industry. These are, basically, the foundation of any business and people might even refer to it as an investment. If done right, this can lead to success and victory. It is a primary starting point if you want your SEO game to be strong alongside your business.

Some people might say creating quality content is easy, but I want you to know it is something you must be prepared for. Quality content, especially consistent quality content, is not easy to produce. It will require much perseverance and attention.

You have to think of unique and brilliant ideas. Take your time and brainstorm, research if you must, and study the topic carefully. If you find it hard then start at the top; an attractive headline.

The moment you start putting your own spin on it, make certain you're not missing any important components that might affect the total presentation of your awesome content.

It doesn't matter if you're new to this or not, there's always a professional way of doing things by improving every day through creating daily posts. From your own starting point, you can improve little by little.

It doesn't really matter if you are a beginner or a professional, because improvement is achieved by growing a little every day through continuous experience. Little by little, you will be better.

Keyword research

Keywords are everything, because no matter how informative the piece you wrote, if you didn't do your keyword research, then no one is going to find it.

Of course, when establishing your own compelling headline, you should include the keyword in it, so readers will know. To enhance your content's visibility, the keyword should be well-apportioned. It should be used a number of times throughout the article.

That covered, remember that, before you start typing away, you need to get your keyword game on point. Now, there are a lot of factors you should consider when you're doing On-Page SEO, but this is the most time-consuming.

Take note: This is the sustenance of your content. You must make sure you have done the proper research and evaluation, and you need to be confident with your keyword research before you can say it's all done and ready to be uploaded to the online world.

Proper Use of Keywords

Have you heard of the 'old keyword stuffing' technique? It was extremely well known in the SEO world, but of course, no longer works.

Because, as we have discussed, Google is getting cleverer as time goes by, they have become much stricter with their regulations. Although I have mentioned that keywords are important in your content, randomly placing those keywords all over your article, or entry, isn't a great idea at all.

Doing so will have a negative effect, specifically on your rankings. And remember, the goal, at the end of the day, is be on the top page of search results.

Going back to the year 2015, the use of keywords revolved around semantics. Here's the creepy part, Google has evolved so much that its algorithm can now effectively interpret the meanings of keywords that people use.

It boils down to the fact that now Google not only takes keywords into consideration, but it also studies the meanings and synonyms of the keyword.

It's not about the quantity of the keywords though, the primary thing you should be concerned with is the proper placement of the keyword. It should be strategically placed, especially in headlines, in the URL, and, of course, the meta description.

So, write quality content for your readers while also being smart about the placement of your keyword.

Post Frequently

Remember I told you that you must create 'CONSISTENT' quality work? Well, I meant it. When I said 'consistently' I didn't mean once every six months. If you post rarely then you shouldn't expect your site's ranking to be boosted higher. Fresher content and an updated site will have a higher chance of success.

If you post frequently, it sends Google the message that you are running a dedicated and serious content site.

If writing new content frequently is hard for you, you can do other things, such as modifying previous posts. Make it more current or provide new information to entice your previous readers into coming back.

I personally know someone who, over the span of three years, has written only six articles. However, she tops the rankings - and no, she didn't use any hocus pocus. Instead, her secret is that she constantly updates her previous articles. She adds new information, new sources, a new twist on the topic featured in the original post. And she does it frequently.

Sure, posting as often as daily, or three times a week is great. But hopefully, you haven't forgotten about maintaining the quality your posts. Remember, every post you write must be worth the read to make the readers keep on coming.

Direct answers

A direct answer is a new factor in SEO. It is something you should pay attention to as well. You must basically make sure that Google is able to analyze what is written in your post.

When Google likes what it sees, and that it is applicable to a certain inquiry, it will generate a good result.

Take, for example, Matt Cutts, the former head of the web spam team at Google. He was also the go-to man for Google's updates on SEO and algorithm.

Just last year, he stated that marketers who cut editing to the bone are on the right track. The 'direct to the point' post is now the key to conquering the SEO field.

In addition, this also means that using fancy words isn't doing your post any favors. Readers want it simple as they do not want to search on Google for definitions as they are reading your post. At the same time, it allows Google's algorithm to understand your content better.

So, as much as possible, refrain from using fancy words the average Joe and Jane would find hard to understand. Not only that, but even though the Google system is much more advanced in so many ways, using simpler words makes it easier for their algorithm to understand your content better.

HTML

You've been doing great; you have systematically followed the SEO content rules, and you are 100% content with what you have created. But hold your horses because you aren't done yet!

There is still a lot more to do. Now, let us focus our attention on HTML. YES! HTML! A lot of people will react badly to this. They might even feel anxiety. What is HTML? How hard is it? Now, before you start saying that you aren't a professional in any way, you must understand you don't need to have a degree in this field to know how to use it.

Just answer this simple question; are you serious about making it big and gaining success in your business? If yes, then you are good to go. All you need to do is spend some time learning the basics of HTML - which is simple.

Why do you need HTML? Imagine you want to bake a moist chocolate cake, but you don't know how to operate an oven. That's a great simile to compare with wanting to be great at SEO but not knowing the basics of HTML.

Thankfully, the internet is a knowledge melting pot! You can learn the basics, for free, while sitting in front of your desktop.

Before we go on to discuss other matters, let's look at the four components of SEO HTML. This should help you a lot in creating a better foundation for the content you have written.

Title Tags

Title tags are very important. They must briefly and accurately describe the topic and theme of your document or post. You will see them in two places. In the top bar of the internet browser, and under the Search Result Pages.

HTML tag are commonly called titles, however, for some blogs, they're called H1-tag. As the name implies, this is the first heading.

To make sure things go smoothly, I recommend your site's page only has a single h1-tag. Google will then understand the message you want to portray better. Make sure it is enticing and accurate at the same time, to make it more effective.

One good thing is that a WordPress SEO plugin, by Yoast, gives you the opportunity to create a custom title tag within the platform.

The best thing to do is to ensure you stay below the character limit, currently 70 characters, before showing ellipses. This way, your titles will be displayed properly. I suggest you try Snippet Optimizer to simulate how your title and meta description will appear in SERP's.

Meta description

The meta description is like the attractive wrapper you use when giving out gifts. The job of a meta description is to attract the readers, so remember this is the first interaction many visitors have with your brand. Make it welcoming.

People who have done proper research regarding SEO, will excel in constructing their meta description. You can spot people who aren't fully matured marketers by the way they tend to end a sentence with the "…" effect.

Another thing to watch out for are people who write an incomplete meta description; meaning they tend to cut it short in the middle. Meanwhile, for newbies, the placement of the keyword is right off the bat.

A lot of people feel pressurized by the length of the meta description. Yoast did say it should have 160 characters as a maximum limit, however, I think it would be best if you don't pressure yourself at the beginning, and instead focus first on the quality, and how creative you can be.

Why? Because you are trying to build a page of quality content. Meaning what you are doing should prioritize in seeking to capture the reader's attention. They are the source of all traffic and sales.

But don't forget, of course, that earlier in 2016, the length of descriptions for desktops, under Google, was 200 characters for the desktop, while mobiles could have up to 172 characters. Oh, and another tip is to check which pages are missing a meta description. The easy way to do so is to run your website through Screaming Frog's SEO Spider. It shows you every URL under your domain, the meta description, and its length.

Schema

One of the lesser known parts of the SEO game is called 'Schema'. This may not be the focus for everyone, however it won't hurt if you learn how it impacts your content. The schema is simply the end-result of the partnership of several search engines.

This could also fall into the category of HTML tags. Remember, this mostly unknown part of SEO can either positively or negatively impact how your piece is being displayed on the results pages of the search engines; it is referred to as SERPS.

To give you some idea, Schema is used for the following most of the time:

- Businesses and organizations
- People
- Products
- Recipes
- Reviews
- Videos

Even though it might be a small factor, it still affects the overall ranking. So it is worth the time to practice and make it a habit.

I hope any fears you might have had when you heard the word 'Schema' have been put to rest.

Schema is much easier to apply than it seems. With proper research and practice, you will be good to go in no time.

Of course, the work may seem tedious, but given time and effort, you'll be certain to reap the benefits from your labor.

Subheads

Try to imagine reading an instructional manual textbook without any sub-headings, can you work with that? Well, yes. However, it would hard and confusing. Having proper subheadings on the subject would make it much better.

Now apply that scenario to your content article/piece. Not having any proper sub-headings would lead to confusion and irritation on your readers' part. Therefore, do make sure you learn how to divide one relevant topic from another.

The good news is that it not only has the role of making sure the format is at its best with a good-looking structure and great content, but it also lifts a heavy weight off your readers as sub-headings provide them with accessible reference points.

Making sure the format is at its best by providing good-looking structure and great content will lead to satisfied readers who have access to reference points.

Not only that, proper sub-heads also give impact on the SEO effect. H1-tags is the major point, but h2, h3, and h4 will also be a huge determining factor in your page's success.

It's not going to be a hassle though. This is pretty easy when you're using WordPress for your SEO game.

Architecture

This will be the last topic that will focus on On-Page SEO. It is all about your site's architecture.

This part may be a bit tricky and confusing, but that's just at the start. The more you learn and experience in your SEO game; the more complicated tricks and ideas you will be able to use and implement on your page.

Here's the thing; a site that has an awesome architecture usually comes with huge advantages. People will love it because it will be easy to navigate the site itself. In addition, loading times will be faster and will also safeguard privacy and connection, and it will also be more accessible to everyone as it would tend to have a mobile-friendly design.

The first thing is to make sure you have a clear idea of what your user wants and needs. In that way, you can build a page architecture format in your mind, even before purchasing your site domain. Doing this will save you wasting time, money, and effort.

After all, to provide an awesome user experience, your site must be easily accessible to your readers and, at the same time, should also be creative.

Your architecture must allow optimization as well. It is important to craft a wonderful search engine experience that will attract people.

If you want to generate positive feedback on Google, and for your page to rank better, you must make your site accessible to users.

Easy to crawl

Nowadays we have programs called 'spiders'. Basically, a spider's job is to crawl from one page to another on your website, and via links.

The crawlers report to Google regarding how they should index your website. So the easier access they have, the better the result for you.

The secret here is that you should have a great, thick web of links visible between the pages of your website. By having this, the spiders can easily crawl from one page to another. In other words, they'll be able to check all of them, and thus they can render a good report to Google, and other search engines, which will ensure they understand your site better.

To make it much easier for Google spiders and readers, you should consider making a sitemap. Using WordPress, and having a basic plugin, can positively affect results.

Duplicate content

And now we shall tackle duplicate content. This subject is extremely sensitive solely because there are so many misconceptions. However, we can try to do our best to check what is right and what is wrong regarding duplicate content.

The first thing to talk about is the common rookie marketer mistake; the mentality that everything on a page should be original. Nothing less but 100 % original.

This isn't necessarily correct in every way. Reposting your own piece on other websites you don't own, or even publishing a post from a guest, won't hurt your ranking level, as long as you don't do it in the same way as spam.

So, for example, if you plan on re-posting the similar content on one of the big outlets on the web, your ranking can be negatively affected.

The reason is simple. Google's priority is towards indexing medium articles because its algorithm deems them to be more credible, more authoritative, and much more reliable.

Mobile-friendliness

Did you know that mobile devices are already in the lead for most internet usage, even outperforming desktop devices? Soon we will live in a world where everything is done via gadgets we can hold in our hand and put in our pockets.

Aodhan Cullen, chief executive of StatCounter, said, "This should be a wakeup call, especially for small businesses, sole traders and professionals, to make sure their websites are mobile friendly. Many older websites are not. Mobile compatibility is increasingly important, not just because of growing traffic, but because Google favors mobile-friendly websites for its mobile search results."

You have a lot of options in the market on how to make your page mobile-friendly. However, I suggest that you first use Google Mobile-Friendly Test to test your website and see which parts of your website need to be fixed and updated.

But you don't really have to feel anxious about this as WordPress themes are now being readily made mobile-friendly. If the chosen theme of your WordPress isn't, you can simply install a plugin, and you're done. Welcome to the mobile future where everything can be found in the palm of your hand.

Page speed

And boom! We wake up one day to find an official statement from Google that page speed will be a ranking factor in its mobile-first index. That means if you want to be on the top, you should work on making your site as fast and accessible as possible.

The guys at Google have released a tool that can give you help on this subject. Also, you can always open up Pingdom to check your page speed.

This is an extremely important factor. It affects both your ranking in the SEO field, and general customer happiness. So yes, I suggest you do it now. No waiting. Make that page move as fast as flash.

After all, if we are going to be honest, people are impatient. I am and so are you. When a person wants something, they want it now.

Two of the most effective ideas on how to make your page faster:

- Audit and monitor all third-party scripts on your site that affect your mobile page speed.
- Limit the number of images per page. As Yoast says, "The image should reflect the topic of the post, or have illustrative purposes within the article, of course."

For SEO purposes, make sure every image you have on your page is scaled correctly. The larger the image, the longer your page will take to load. Put simply, the heavier your bag is, the slower you move, right? Scale the image appropriately, and make sure it shows in the smallest possible size.

We're living in a world where people need to take a picture of their lunch before eating, so yes, pictures will play a huge part. So, while content is the most important, make sure your images are not bad to look at as well.

Keywords in URLs

So here we go again with how important keywords can be in the field of SEO. If you remember, I told you how crucial keywords are and, of course, their proper placement. One of the places that keywords should be is in the URL.

And again, let me emphasize, "THIS IS REALLY IMPORTANT". There! I hope that drives the message in, because if you want your SEO ranking to increase, you must pay attention to this point. And, of course, you should also think about customizing the format that you have with your permalinks.

Here is a tip: There are different types of keyword. You must choose which one is most appropriate.

- Informational Keywords: These are direct to the point keywords like, "on-page SEO", when a user wants to learn more about that specific topic.
- Transactional Keywords: These are would-be words that address users who are looking to buy a product or service. Typically, they include adjectives like 'best' or 'top'.

- Location-Based Keywords: These are used when users are looking for a local business or a specific physical location.

HTTPS and SSL

What are HTTPS and SSL? Well HTTPS stands for Hyper Text Transfer Protocol, while SSL stands for Secure Sockets Layer.

Both are going to be equally worth your time and having either of these will give you a minor ranking boost.

And, even though it is just a minor boost, it could help you a lot if you're involved in a tiebreaker ranking match between your page and someone else's.

Google's Webmaster Trends Analyst Gary Illyes explains it, "If all quality signals are equal for two results, then the one that is on HTTPS would get ... or may get ... the extra boost that is needed to trump the other result."

And if that isn't enough reason for you, then please remember that, aside from ranking, what we should value above all else is the satisfaction of our customers. And the people who visit your page want to know you are concerned about their privacy as well.

It's much better if, before you purchase your domain, you include, as one of your options on the web hosting service, the SSL – HTTPS.

So that's it for the main factors of On-Page SEO. Now let's go through a mini checklist, shall we?

- Is your content original? How can a quality page support and publish plagiarized work? Make sure you use Copyscape.
- Is your content useful to readers? Are you writing something that people can relate to and use in daily life?
- Is your content well researched? Is that information and data valid? Do you have references? 'No' to articles that spread fake news.
- Do you have a smart and effective publishing strategy?
- The page titles you use on every page - are they different and creative enough to entice?
- Is your text properly formatted? Make sure you put to good use H1, H2, Bold, and Italics.
- Are you using pictures with image filenames that are descriptive enough?

- Are your posts and pages grouped into categories already?
- Do you utilize the 'Related Posts' section at the end of each page?

Always remember that On-Page SEO is not about manipulating your website to please Google's algorithm. In some ways that is still the case, but Google's algorithm is much smarter now and has become more and more advanced. The focus of SEO is shifting to a more reliable and credible purpose of pleasing the user and engaging them in natural ways, and that, my friend, is your goal.

CHAPTER 7

⌒

Perks of Off-Page SEO

SEO doesn't only apply within your website, SEO happens all over the internet. Let's talk about how Off-Page can positively affect your business and company in general.

Reliance

Naturally, you will have already heard about the ever-famous formula that has been created by the big-time CEO's of Google, which we now consider as PageRank. But that's not the only consideration that tells Google who deserves to be on the list of the top ten websites.

Currently, there are many online entrepreneurs who are only looking at this business short-term, which mainly explains why there are a lot of spammy and non-relevant websites on the internet these days. In fact, they have been rampant.

Alain Magnuson

Because of the numbers of websites that are considered unworthy and unreliable, trust is now a big factor in this SEO game – so yes, it affects your ranking.

Google has created TrustRank, and this is how Google deals with the incredible number of sites that are making their way onto the world wide web. Through TrustRank, they'll be able to verify whether your site is genuine with its content or not.

Naturally, if the company or business you own is one of the big-timers in the game, then obviously, search engines will trust you more than those sites that aren't.

Including high-quality backlinks within your content that comes from authority, search engines will give you higher chances of ranking on the top page. These sites usually end with .edu and .gov domains.

Let's talk more about the matter at hand and check out the other components that make up your reliability, or trustworthiness, to the search engines.

Authority

In a nutshell, search engines will judge your site as one of the two kinds of authority you'll be able to forge.

The first is the domain authority. This is when your domain popularity is off-the-charts. For instance, we have apple.com as one of the most authoritative domains of the day.

The second is page authority. This does not focus on the entire domain, but on the popularity of the page and the quality of the content.

Bounce Rate

'Bounce rate' is often overlooked by new online entrepreneurs. Sure, getting traffic is important, and it's your primary goal, but you have to make sure your site is informative enough for the audience to want to stay and read your content.

Bounce rate is determined by the audience who visit your website, take a look at a page for only a couple of seconds, and then leave.

When this happens, Google automatically assumes that, although your site is getting traffic, you're not doing a good job at creating high-quality content that causes people to 'stick' and read your blog or content.

Of course, there are other things you have to think about, like the loading time of your site and navigation.

It's not rocket science, if you want Google to recognize your page as an authority, then create a blog that keeps your readers interested in what you're telling them, while making sure you have fast loading times and a proper appearance.

Do this consistently and Google will start to notice your page and place you higher in the rankings.

Domain age

Age plays a huge part in your website reliability. Just as we tend to listen to people who are older than we are, the age of your domain also plays a role in driving traffic and allowing your audience to trust your content.

The algorithm of some search engines, like Google, tends to rank domains that are older, higher in the results. If you haven't bought a domain as yet, then investing time and money to look for domains that have already expired is definitely worth the effort. Successful online marketers do it all the time!

Identity

It's always a major trust booster when you have an identity to prove your reliability or track record, and, even in the online world, it plays a huge part. Owning a brand of your own will indicate to Google, and other search engines, that you are the real deal.

There's a way to find out if you are doing well in your business. If you already have an existing brand, try to look it up on a search engine. If something pops up about your site, then you are well on your way to success.

Creating a brand doesn't necessarily mean using a different name, there are a lot of online gurus whose brand is their own personal name – the result is just as good.

Pro Tip: Focusing on building a brand helps a lot as it will play a part in preventing your site from future updates in regards to search engine penalties.

Links

I've stressed the importance of backlinks in the earlier portion of this e-Book; however, it doesn't mean that having backlinks will guarantee a successful SEO journey.

Links play a part in the SEO hustle, and there are a variety of ways in which you'll be able to have backlinks. Just to remind you, waiting for marketers to link to your site may take a while, so taking the initiative to move will help your business a lot.

Link Quality – As always, link quality will always triumph over link quantity. In the past, there have been a lot of marketers who have attempted to put a ton of links within their content thinking they would rank better.

WRONG.

This will actually hurt your rankings more than anything else. Take time to search for high-quality links. It's better not to link at all if you're not sure whether you are linking to the right site for your source.

Anchor Text – this is the text used when other sites are linking to your website. The types of anchor text are quite easy to identify; if there's anything you need to focus on, it is keeping the anchor text natural.

In other words, it should be read within your content in a natural flow. People who have only just started focusing on SEO have a tendency to put 'click here' as the text – the same thing I did back when I initially started out.

As you go on with your SEO experience, you'll get more experience in how you can naturally create anchor text in your content.

Personal

Let's move on to Personal, as there are some things you don't have the power to control. I'll be sharing some of the ways you can add some tweaks here and there to take advantage of this topic.

Country – Google, along with other search engines, have been programmed to only show results that are beneficial to the person asking the question. Meaning they want the searcher to find what they need within their country.

Try to type anything on Google - let's say a place where you want to eat, or a service - you'll see how Google will only show the stores that are within your time zone.

What's more, the Google algorithm knows the differences between particular words.

In addition, Google's algorithm is also well-aware of the differences of specific words in some other countries. For instance, if you are in the US, the word 'comforter' translates to bed blankets.

However, in the UK, if you type in the same keyword, what you're going to see is a list of pacifiers. The reason is simple;

it's because it's because words can mean different things in different countries.

That fact alone can tell you a lot about what Google is all about, and through the years, they have become quite specific in what the searcher needs.

If you're looking for information in a particular country, make sure to specify it when you're typing the keyword.

City – Search Engines have become even more specific in recent years. These engines do not only have the capacity to track the country you're residing in, but can also drill down to a city-level, thanks to its geo-targeting.

Let's say you want something to eat and you're looking for a fast food restaurant that can deliver. Type the keyword and Google will show you results for restaurants that are near to your location.

Searcher's history – If you have a reader that frequently visits your site, and that person is looking for information on a particular topic that you've created content about, the search engine will automatically place your site on the first page of the search.

Socialization – Getting a boost from other sources can help your business a lot, especially if you put in enough time to drive traffic to your site as well as sales.

YouTube has become a popular platform for advertisements and informative content about your company. Growing your subscriber count will enable you to gain a following. You can also go the extra mile and build your Google Plus Profile as well.

When someone follows your brand, for instance, on YouTube, then the search engines will automatically assume that person likes your content. Hence, they will be shown more of what you have to offer when they look it up on the search bar.

Social

Social signals have an effect on search engines, so if you want to rank better, consider these two factors to help you out to find out how you can manipulate traffic to your benefit.

Share Quality – In the area of digital marketing, the quality of 'shares' is an important factor that determines the success of your posting. This simply means the person who shared your content has a social impact on your credibility.

Google has already identified who the people are that have made a name in the industry – just as Twitter knows who has made a name in a specified business by using a verified check mark.

I'll show you an example: Let's say someone with a big name has shared your post - like Mark Zuckerberg. Not only will people start to notice your posting more through his shared post, but Google will also look at it as high-quality content.

Of course, you may see getting big-time influencers to share your posts as a bit difficult. However, you can always increase the chances of being shared, by shooting them an e-mail about your upcoming content and how it may be relevant to them.

Or you could be smart in your approach by asking them for an interview, or by quoting them. This way, they'll be able to promote themselves through your post, and, at the same time, they'll also boost your reputation. It's a win-win situation.

Pro Tip: Hook up with Topsy, it's a well-known plug that gives you details on who the top influencers are that might want to read about your topic.

Share Quantity – If you can't get an influencer to share your post, then you can always fight it out with the number of shares. In other words, you'll have to start an internet trend.

When people start sharing your content like it's a new viral post, search engines will favor your content. Here's the thing; although becoming viral is somewhat easy these days, it's not a sure-fire thing.

You always have to keep in mind that people on the internet are looking for quality, witty posts that are relatable. So, if you want to have a shot at winning the quantity game, just be consistent with your postings.

CHAPTER 8

~

Earning Through Blogging

Blogging and earning may sound too good to be true, however, it has been done by millions of online marketers all over the world.

The problem is that, although that there are millions who have made a stable income through blogging, there are billions of others who have failed miserably in their attempts to live a dream life.

Here's the key to winning at blogging, even if you keep losing: Blog on a topic that you're truly passionate about.

If you're blogging on a niche that you're REALLY into, and you simply want to share what you have to say to other people, then you're going to win the SEO game.

One thing I have learned from my years of experience in writing blogs is that building your site is not a race – it's a marathon.

Keeping your mindset on the right track allows you to see clearly the positive light of building a blog. It's a rewarding experience.

Successful entrepreneurs, like Neil Patel, didn't start out as big-time professionals. Consistency is what made Neil who he is - together with quality content.

Achieving only a couple of hundreds of visitors a month can be your gateway to getting five million readers on a yearly basis. There are a couple of factors to consider when you're planning to start your own blog.

Here is what you need to think about:

Blogging Topics

Topics are pretty much hard to find. Probably one of the hardest things you have to think about before you can actually start typing away your fears is what topic you want to discuss.

There are bloggers who already know what they are going for, and they typically succeed more than those who don't.

Don't get me wrong, it doesn't mean you're clueless about what you're trying to get into, or that you are already a hopeless cause. There are tons of popular bloggers who have started out with no clear direction on what they want to tackle, and that's okay.

People have different reasons why they want to write – it's either that they're passionate about something and they want to share, or they simply want to try out various areas of their life.

It doesn't matter what your reason is, you always have to keep in mind: **Only build on a niche you don't mind writing about for years to come.**

If you're just like me, someone who doesn't know what topic to start with, or you don't have any authority over the niche of your choice, then you can simply start to write what's on your mind anyway.

Topics may be as complex as science, physics, and technology, or it could be as simple as writing about your favorite games, product reviews, and babies.

Domain Name

I've talked about domain names in the earlier portion of the e-Book, but we'll dig a little deeper on the subject now. To be honest, thinking of a domain name can be an undeniably fun task, especially if you have a group of people with you who'll help you come up with a fun name.

Since there are billions of websites on the internet, we can't deny the fact competition isn't the easiest around. This is especially true if you plan to purchase a domain with .com as the extension. Chances are, the domain name has already been bought by someone.

Of course, your options aren't limited. There are currently 486 extensions that you can choose from, such as .com, or net, etc.

Pro Tip: Make the domain name easy to remember for the users so that they can type it easily into the search bar.

There are situations where a user will accidentally type the wrong domain name because of the complexity of the name. When this happens, you're deliberately giving traffic to your competitors, which could cause potential losses.

CHAPTER 9

Amazon Affiliate Marketing and SEO

First things first; what is 'affiliate marketing'? It is simply a link in a page and click that takes you to a website where you can buy a product or service. This is one of the options of earning money online. And people have been telling their success stories specifically about being Amazon affiliates.

People swear there are instances where you only need to sell two or three items a day via Amazon affiliated links to cross the $100/day threshold.

One of the good things here is that starting an Amazon Affiliate Website is easy. The Amazon 'cookie' allows you to gain profit from other products besides the one you're promoting, and you don't have to do much 'selling'. Review posts generates good traffic, and there are lots of opportunities, especially for a good product.

Moving forward, you must remember that for an Amazon affiliate site to work, you're going to need three things:

1. Solid Targeted Traffic

Whether you own a blog site, run a digital marketing agency or sell programs and software, you need content that brings in targeted traffic.

Targeted traffic means traffic that converts into leads and sales. To be successful in this area you should make sure you have 'The Right Content'. Remember the following points:

- Publishing content that appeals to your target customer isn't enough. You need content that your influencers want to share with their audiences.
- You need to know what topics influencers care most about.
- Appealing content is a must.
- Include 'Share Triggers' in your content. Share triggers are scientifically-backed psychological principles that, when included in your content, embolden people to share.

2. A High Price Series of Products to Promote

If you're primarily going to be promoting Amazon products, it's important to choose a set of products that have a relatively high price point. After all, it's hard to make a solid income by promoting $1-5 products with a price tag between one and five dollars since the commission on Amazon is so low. Items that have a higher price point, like high-end appliances, furniture, BBQ's, blenders, juicers, or bikes, can net you over $50 for each sale.

There are a number of high-priced Amazon products that cost up to six figures. You can promote these as an affiliate if you research well. Remember, one of the famous con's (as opposed to 'pro's) of Amazon is that they have low commission rates. That said, you will see you need to be promoting expensive products.

But if you can't find a high-end series of products you'd like to promote, then try promoting cheaper products that have a high volume.

Bear in mind, the Amazon cookie stays active for 24 hours. Which means you'll receive an affiliate commission for any products that are bought during that period.

3. Niche Selection

This is the most crucial part. To help you out you can try using Google's External Keyword Tool. This will help you find the right keywords to work with. After deciding on the keyword, it is best to check how competitive that keyword is. But don't afraid of competition! You can always defeat it with vigor and passion.

How to set up an Amazon affiliate site with Wordpress

I will be concentrating on WordPress since this is the most common, and easiest, way to start an SEO page.

- Choose a domain name – Choose one that will give a definitive domain that will not limit you to a specific area so you will always have wider potential for your website in the future. Don't choose things like 'topgrillreview'. What if, in the future, you aren't about grills anymore? Online success today is all about long-term thinking.
- Pick a Web Host – A web host is the entity that keeps all the files needed to make sure your site functions well. Some will be dedicated towards sites with large volumes of traffic, while others will specifically host WordPress sites.

- Install WordPress – Nowadays, most web hosts make it very easy to install WordPress on your new site. Some even offer a one-click install that guides you through the entire process. So do your research well, and make sure you have all the tools and plugins for your WordPress site.

How to create solid Amazon affiliate content

1. The Extensive Review Post

This is one of the posts you will write a lot about. Take note it will act as a piece of sales copy to convince your visitor to head over to Amazon.

This post should provide your buyer with all they need to know about the product to help them make their buying decision. You will find a few of the ingredients you'll want to include in each post below:

- Make sure you connect with your reader by targeting their 'pain points'.
- Point out the pros and cons of the product, but make sure you talk about why the pros are greater than the cons.
- Focus on the benefits of each product feature.

- Product description should be on point.
- Give your final verdict; and make sure you include your affiliate link.

2. The Comparison Post

For a comparison post, you'll typically distinguish between, and contrast two or more products. Your goal here is not to make one better than the other, but to highlight how the two differ, and how they can serve the different needs of different customers.

- Choose the products to compare.
- Research the products carefully. You need to know the pros and cons, the features, warranty details, and more. If you don't know much about the products, how can you compare them right?
- Make sure you use a catchy title. A good title is already strong promotional work. The title is the first thing people see after all, so if it isn't interesting, they won't bother.
- And, here comes the daunting part. . . writing. It is a huge factor- a lot of the success will depend strongly on your writing style and how you present the data to your readers.

- Is the title already catchy? Make sure you also end your post with a bang! A great closing statement that leaves an impression on your readers is a must.

3. The How-To Post

It is extremely constructive to publish helpful posts that target your specific market. For instance, if your site is dedicated to dogs, you could create posts that cover topics like:

- Five Main Things to Know About Taking Care of Dogs
- The Best Guide on How to Treat Your Dog
- How to Tell if a Dog Is in Pain
- How to Give Your Dog a Bath

4. Roundup and Listicle Posts

Listicle posts are taking over the internet. They are shared a lot, so they have the chance to bring a lot of traffic back to your website and, at the same time, attract relevant links to help improve your search engine rankings. But yes, this post is going to take a lot of time, effort, and patience to research the topic at hand. But the pain will be worth the gain at the end of the day.

Here are some of the most successful Amazon Affiliate Websites out there:

ThisIsWhyImBroke.com

This website focuses on the coolest gadgets, gifts, tech, and oddities from Amazon and around the web..

Monthly Visitors (SimilarWeb): 2.4 million visitors

Average Post Length: 10 – 160 words

How much do they make: Around $20,000+ per month from Amazon

TheWirecutter.com

This website features reviews from independent reviewers. They inform readers they receive commissions but provide honest comments. And I love this website for the sole reason that they believe, and put into action, the 'content is king' strategy.

Monthly Visitors (SimilarWeb): 8.10 million visitors

Average Post Length: 3,000 - 5,000 words

How much do they make: In 2015, this site, combined with The Wirecutter, made $150 million in e-commerce sales. So you can get an idea of their commission revenue.

BabyGearLab.com

This website targeted two things people can't resist; reading reviews and babies! They capture readers attention, especially parents, by reviewing baby stuff and making it understandable.

Monthly Visitors (SimilarWeb): 234,100 visitors
Average Post Length: 6,000 - 10,000 words

ConsumerSearch.com

This website has been active for more than ten years simply reviewing different products. They started around the year 2000. Imagine how successful a website is to have that kind of longevity.

Monthly Visitors (SimilarWeb): 1.10 million visitors
Average Post Length: 1,000 words
How much do they make: This site was bought for $33 Million from About.com in 2007.

TheSweetHome.com

This website is not afraid of posting long reviews. They have one soda stream review that contained over 13,000 words. Imagine that?

Monthly Visitors (SimilarWeb): 2.5 million visitors

Average Post Length: 4,000 – 5,000 words

How much do they make: In 2015, this site, combined with The Wirecutter made $150 million in e-commerce sales. So you can get an idea of their commission revenue.

CHAPTER 10

◦

Writing Search-Optimized Review Articles

The only persuasive power you have to convince your readers is your content. As an affiliate marketer, you only have one goal: Make them click your affiliate link!

While that may sound like a breeze, outranking the top ten niche sites for your designated keywords is not that easy to do. But it's definitely not impossible.

However, you do need to bust your ass to produce high-quality review articles. Content must be 100% original.

Since we are in this post-panda age, spinning and rehashing your content is going to mean your site will be lost in the SEO rankings. Besides, plagiarism is totally uncool.

Make your readers spend more time on your niche site by providing them with valuable information – do hours of content research, exert every effort in writing captivating copy - and the rankings will follow.

There are a number of things I want to talk to you about, so let's get started with...

- **Don't be a Salesman**

Or just don't be 'cringy'.

There's a huge difference between 'informing' and 'selling' when writing product reviews. The funny thing is, writing in a 'sales' way (much like Amazon's product descriptions) doesn't really work well for a lot of niche site owners.

But hey – people still do it. Well, at least there are turnkey vendors out there that basically don't make any effort to create their own review. Copying descriptions straight off Amazon isn't really a smart move. Obviously!

Main point: DON'T BE THAT GUY!

Visitors are after your professional opinion, they want a realistic overview of what they can expect when the product is delivered to their door.

Tip: Talk about all the areas you would want to know about if you were the buyer.

- **Don't Use Unexciting Products**

You want to build a credible website where visitors can learn to trust your product recommendations, and choosing unpopular items with almost no reviews on Amazon will kill your objective.

Recommend products that Amazon would consider 'Best Sellers'. Personally, I go through a long list of products on Amazon, and make sure they have the following:

- POSITIVE REVIEWS. This helps you write compelling copy that sells – don't write just for the sake of having something 'nice' to say.
- RECOMMENDATIONS. If the product has been recommended by a number of credible niche sites, and the feedback is good, it's a keeper.

In connection with (2), there's a neat trick I use when I'm looking for sellable products. I would look into several affiliate sites that target the same niche as me and take a look at their product references.

For instance, if I were to write about gaming gears (keyboards, mouse, chairs, etc.) I would check out **HannaSeo** for ideas. This makes my job way easier, and it saves me a ton of time on product research.

- **Tell Them What They Want to Hear**

Apparently, readers aren't too keen on hearing about the product's features. Your site's visitors want to know what's in it for them – in other words, how would the product benefit them?

Let's talk about facts, about **81% of buyers do online research** before making the big purchase. And there's at least 60% of people who base that decision to buy on search engine results.

Just as I mentioned earlier, they do not want to see Amazon bullet-pointed features.

Put some meat on your statement; inform them, tell them what they're getting. Take note of the things you think are beneficial for the reader.

Explain each of the features that the product offers, and tell them how they're going to benefit from that feature. Keep it short and simple, just enough for them to visualize the possibilities.

Let's say this is the feature: *It has a 90 to 180-degree backward movement – and then you're going to add – making it possible for you to comfortably lie down, just as you can in a bed.*

Another thing to keep in mind when writing a product review is to show them the pros and cons. Just mention the things you liked and disliked about the product.

Writing the cons is super important as we want to leave the reader with the impression that we're unbiased and genuine with our review. There is no such thing as a perfect product.

But you still have to make sure the good outweighs the bad. After all, we're here to make sales.

- **Fifth-Graders Should be Able to Understand**

Please don't use unnecessarily big words when writing your review. In the first place, we might just be talking about something like rocking chairs, for Pete's sake! No need to bring your dictionary out.

Just write in the way you would normally talk to a person – no complicated, fancy words. Especially as we're here to sell products to the general population, not to impress our professor.

Keeping it simple speaks volumes to the readers.

Use words you know they will be able to understand.

But using simple words isn't enough, you must create engaging content. As I said, there's no point in making your review sound like you're reading a class report. Write the way you talk, casually – it ALWAYS works!

- **Research Your Product Thoroughly**

Sure, researching isn't exactly the best, most interesting part of the job, but it is certainly one of the most crucial.

If you want to beat the Top Ten Niche Sites targeting your keyword, then you had better prepare to research your content. For hours!

You don't want to give inaccurate information and facts, right? Prioritizing your site's credibility comes first - more than anything else.

Writers often make the common mistake of basing their research material on a single source. It isn't enough! Take advantage of the internet and go crazy.

Read reviews on Amazon; stalk the company's website; check out authority sites for more information, and, if it's still insufficient, look for video reviews on YouTube.